This journal belongs to

"The LORD make His face shine on you, And be gracious to you;" - Numbers 6:25

"The LORD make His face shine on you, And be gracious to you;" - Numbers 6:25

"The LORD make His face shine on you, And be gracious to you;" - Numbers 6:25

"The LORD make His face shine on you, And be gracious to you;" - Numbers 6:25

"The LORD make His face shine on you, And be gracious to you;" - Numbers 6:25

"The LORD make His face shine on you, And be gracious to you;" - Numbers 6:25

"The LORD make His face shine on you, And be gracious to you;" - Numbers 6:25

"The LORD make His face shine on you, And be gracious to you;" - Numbers 6:25

"The LORD make His face shine on you, And be
gracious to you;" - Numbers 6:25

"The LORD make His face shine on you, And be gracious to you;" - Numbers 6:25

"The LORD make His face shine on you, And be gracious to you;" - Numbers 6:25

"The LORD make His face shine on you, And be gracious to you;" - Numbers 6:25

"The LORD make His face shine on you, And be gracious to you;" - Numbers 6:25

"The LORD make His face shine on you, And be gracious to you;" - Numbers 6:25

"The LORD make His face shine on you, And be gracious to you;" - Numbers 6:25

"The LORD make His face shine on you, And be gracious to you;" - Numbers 6:25

"The LORD make His face shine on you, And be
gracious to you;" - Numbers 6:25

"The LORD make His face shine on you, And be gracious to you;" - Numbers 6:25

"The LORD make His face shine on you, And be gracious to you;" - Numbers 6:25

"The LORD make His face shine on you, And be gracious to you;" - Numbers 6:25

"The LORD make His face shine on you, And be gracious to you;" - Numbers 6:25

"The LORD make His face shine on you, And be gracious to you;" - Numbers 6:25

"The LORD make His face shine on you, And be gracious to you;" - Numbers 6:25

"The LORD make His face shine on you, And be gracious to you;" - Numbers 6:25

"The LORD make His face shine on you, And be gracious to you;" - Numbers 6:25

"The LORD make His face shine on you, And be gracious to you;" - Numbers 6:25

"The LORD make His face shine on you, And be gracious to you;" - Numbers 6:25

"The LORD make His face shine on you, And be gracious to you;" - Numbers 6:25

"The LORD make His face shine on you, And be gracious to you;" - Numbers 6:25

"The LORD make His face shine on you, And be gracious to you;" - Numbers 6:25

"The LORD make His face shine on you, And be gracious to you;" - Numbers 6:25

"The LORD make His face shine on you, And be gracious to you;" - Numbers 6:25

"The LORD make His face shine on you, And be gracious to you;" - Numbers 6:25

"The LORD make His face shine on you, And be gracious to you;" - Numbers 6:25

"The LORD make His face shine on you, And be gracious to you;" - Numbers 6:25

"The LORD make His face shine on you, And be gracious to you;" - Numbers 6:25

"The LORD make His face shine on you, And be gracious to you;" - Numbers 6:25

"The LORD make His face shine on you, And be gracious to you;" - Numbers 6:25

"The LORD make His face shine on you, And be gracious to you;" - Numbers 6:25

"The LORD make His face shine on you, And be gracious to you;" - Numbers 6:25

"The LORD make His face shine on you, And be gracious to you;" - Numbers 6:25

"The LORD make His face shine on you, And be gracious to you;" - Numbers 6:25

"The LORD make His face shine on you, And be
gracious to you;" - Numbers 6:25

"The LORD make His face shine on you, And be gracious to you;" - Numbers 6:25

"The LORD make His face shine on you, And be gracious to you;" - Numbers 6:25

"The LORD make His face shine on you, And be gracious to you;" - Numbers 6:25

"The LORD make His face shine on you, And be gracious to you;" - Numbers 6:25

"The LORD make His face shine on you, And be gracious to you;" - Numbers 6:25

"The LORD make His face shine on you, And be gracious to you;" - Numbers 6:25

"The LORD make His face shine on you, And be gracious to you;" - Numbers 6:25

"The LORD make His face shine on you, And be gracious to you;" - Numbers 6:25

"The LORD make His face shine on you, And be gracious to you;" - Numbers 6:25

"The LORD make His face shine on you, And be gracious to you;" - Numbers 6:25

"The LORD make His face shine on you, And be gracious to you;" - Numbers 6:25

"The LORD make His face shine on you, And be gracious to you;" - Numbers 6:25

"The LORD make His face shine on you, And be gracious to you;" - Numbers 6:25

"The LORD make His face shine on you, And be gracious to you;" - Numbers 6:25

"The LORD make His face shine on you, And be gracious to you;" - Numbers 6:25

"The LORD make His face shine on you, And be gracious to you;" - Numbers 6:25

"The LORD make His face shine on you, And be gracious to you;" - Numbers 6:25

"The LORD make His face shine on you, And be gracious to you;" - Numbers 6:25

"The LORD make His face shine on you, And be gracious to you;" - Numbers 6:25

"The LORD make His face shine on you, And be
gracious to you;" - Numbers 6:25

"The LORD make His face shine on you, And be gracious to you;" - Numbers 6:25

"The LORD make His face shine on you, And be gracious to you;" - Numbers 6:25

"The LORD make His face shine on you, And be gracious to you;" - Numbers 6:25

"The LORD make His face shine on you, And be gracious to you;" - Numbers 6:25

"The LORD make His face shine on you, And be gracious to you;" - Numbers 6:25

"The LORD make His face shine on you, And be gracious to you;" - Numbers 6:25

"The LORD make His face shine on you, And be gracious to you;" - Numbers 6:25

"The LORD make His face shine on you, And be gracious to you;" - Numbers 6:25

"The LORD make His face shine on you, And be gracious to you;" - Numbers 6:25

"The LORD make His face shine on you, And be gracious to you;" - Numbers 6:25

"The LORD make His face shine on you, And be
gracious to you;" - Numbers 6:25

"The LORD make His face shine on you, And be gracious to you;" - Numbers 6:25

"The LORD make His face shine on you, And be gracious to you;" - Numbers 6:25

"The LORD make His face shine on you, And be gracious to you;" - Numbers 6:25

"The LORD make His face shine on you, And be gracious to you;" - Numbers 6:25

"The LORD make His face shine on you, And be gracious to you;" - Numbers 6:25

"The LORD make His face shine on you, And be gracious to you;" - Numbers 6:25

"The LORD make His face shine on you, And be gracious to you;" - Numbers 6:25

"The LORD make His face shine on you, And be gracious to you;" - Numbers 6:25

"The LORD make His face shine on you, And be gracious to you;" - Numbers 6:25

"The LORD make His face shine on you, And be gracious to you;" - Numbers 6:25

"The LORD make His face shine on you, And be gracious to you;" - Numbers 6:25

"The LORD make His face shine on you, And be
gracious to you;" - Numbers 6:25

"The LORD make His face shine on you, And be gracious to you;" - Numbers 6:25

"The LORD make His face shine on you, And be gracious to you;" - Numbers 6:25

"The LORD make His face shine on you, And be gracious to you;" - Numbers 6:25

"The LORD make His face shine on you, And be gracious to you;" - Numbers 6:25

"The LORD make His face shine on you, And be gracious to you;" - Numbers 6:25

"The LORD make His face shine on you, And be gracious to you;" - Numbers 6:25

"The LORD make His face shine on you, And be gracious to you;" - Numbers 6:25

"The LORD make His face shine on you, And be gracious to you;" - Numbers 6:25

"The LORD make His face shine on you, And be gracious to you;" - Numbers 6:25

"The LORD make His face shine on you, And be gracious to you;" - Numbers 6:25

If you have enjoyed using this journal,
I would greatly appreciate a review.

Thank you, and God bless!

.